20 Tips for a 20-Year-Old

Deanna, you've been putting up
with me and have been a great
mother from my eyes the
whole time (exactly the type of
mom of my girlfriend I expected
to have)

TAYLOR DEL GIUDICE

You and Jason both make
sure Rebeck and Ryan go
there best and I think you've
been the best parents you
could be! — Taylor

ISBN: 978-1-9994145-0-4

This book is dedicated to everyone that came before me and will come after me.

A special thanks to Tessa Jordan and Matthew Tam for their guidance and support

As well as Rebecca for always being there for me no matter what and helping me become the person I am and will become in the future

Contents

Why Read "20 Tips for A 20-Year-Old"?

Real Shit

This book isn't about being nice and avoiding topics. This is about getting the things you want in life, as well as all the hurdles along the way. Each chapter goes in-depth and analyzes the habits and behaviours that we all have; some of which you may not be utilizing. To help you become the person you want to be, you will be taught how to change your own mind, as well as how to make small, but positive changes.

Experiences

All events and tips referenced in this book are from real-life experiences and real advice given to the author throughout his youth. Some of you may have already started applying some of these tips but need an extra push to realize that you matter; this is that extra push. The author of this book found inspiration to write and help others during the author's first-year attending college at British Columbia's Institute of Technology.

Advice from the best

What does advice from the best mean? Well, it means that the author has gathered some of the best available advice from the likes of Gary Vaynerchuk, Grant Cardone, Dale Carnegie, and others. Many of these people have written multiple books, and Gary himself is one of the most well-known entrepreneurs on the planet. He has also created a lot of content around topics mentioned in this book. The advice they give out on a DAILY average is amazing and recommended to be looked at. This book includes some of the best advice and what can be done right now if you put your mind to it.

1

Find Your Passion

People around me always told me that we had to go to school, get a day job, and work till the day we retire. I grew up being told that at home and at school, as well as from friends and everyone else I knew. I quickly realized that life isn't about that. You soon find out that now, you should be finding your own vocation. Now they're telling you that it should be something that you like to do. Now you have to do a 180-degree spin on what you planned and find out what you love to do. What's this now? How does this have anything to do with getting a better life? Let me explain.

You will never be happy with life until you make yourself happy first. If you are comfortable working every day at a job from 9-5 – there isn't anything wrong with that – it must be your passion. Here is a quote from Gary Vaynerchuk, a mogul of social media, and one of the great entrepreneurs of our time: "I'm the happiest because I'm doing exactly what I want to do." This man knew what he wanted to do and pushed everything he had towards it. He found out what his passion was and created a life around that. He made himself happy by doing everything he could do, just to have a life that only encompassed what he loves. Sometimes you might think that you can't create a life around your passion. Let me tell you this: if a person can make up to $12 million in one year by taking videos of himself and doing the things he loves, then you can also make anything out of your own passion while making money.

We get trapped into a certain state of thought, and I believe that is what holds you back. Your friends and family around you tell you that you can't do something and that derails you from your dreams. I want to tell you exactly how to find your passion:

1. Stop giving a fuck about everyone else
2. Repeat

That is what will help you find yourself. If you want to live your best life, then you must stop worrying about what other people tell you and start listening to your own head and what it's trying to tell you. Start looking for any mentors you could have or look for people who are the best at what you want to do. They can help you and you should listen to them.

I know everyone has doubts sometimes, but that is how you find out just how much you want something. Sir Robert Bryson Hall II (otherwise known as Logic) spent every day working two jobs, but he would always go home to work on his craft. Would you be willing to spend your only extra time every day on what you love? I think that if you aren't, then you aren't as passionate about it as you think you are. Now that isn't to say that you don't want it, but you're just not making sure you spend as much time as you should be on it. You're possibly making excuses as to why not to do it or filling your time by going out to the bar. I know that these things are fun to do, as I've had my fair share. My advice to you is to get out of that world. What has the bar done for you, other than suck your wallet dry, and having you think in the morning that you won't be going back there ever again.

Self-audit is a great way to create a path to your passion without annoyances. This will open your eyes to what you should keep doing and stop doing immediately. Focusing on the internal self helps a lot in the external landscape. If you fill each day with activities that benefit you, you will notice that it will only result in upward achievement. Don't think that celebrities are only spending time going out and partying, or better yet, that hip hop artists are spending time out in clubs for no reason. Most of the time, they are making money and not spending money. This also has come from hours and hours in a studio creating music that couldn't be done unless they spent the countless amount of time doing this.

I want you to spend some time and look at what you do daily. Pick out some of the things that you could stop doing that aren't bringing you up. These include:

- Your friends who put you down
- Going out to parties every weekend
- Spending time watching other people do great things and not acting yourself
- "Chillin'"

Cut the word "Chillin'" out of your vocabulary if you use it. This implies that you are not working or sitting on your ass. I absolutely hate that word. Anyways, back to what I was saying.

Find your passion. YOUR passion. Like I said earlier, this isn't about anyone else. No person on this planet is the same, and that goes for what we decide to do in the life that you're so fortunate to live. This generation and what comes after has an opportunity to do anything we want to (See Chapter 9). That is a gift we can't look to waste. The means of creating a stable career out of whatever we want to do is there and that wasn't the case 50 years ago. Whether that be from the phone in your pocket or the fact that you can grow a business without having to spend thousands of dollars on TV advertisements. I want you to answer these simple questions and start looking at how you act on a daily basis. It will help you figure out exactly what it is that you need to be doing to get closer to the day that you wake up and know that you're always going to be happy, no matter what happens.

Questions:

What is it I like to do on a daily basis and would love to get paid for it, if not already getting paid?

What can I do to learn more about it and/or work for someone already doing it?

Write down 3 goals you have for the next couple days you want to achieve. This will help you start your journey and get you into the mood of setting goals.

1.
2.
3.

2

Start Setting Goals

I think this idea is part of the reason why some of the most financially wealthy people on this planet have gotten to the position they are in. We don't know if this works until you start doing it on a regular basis. If you were to ask a random sample of 10 people about if they set monthly goals, you would get an answer of "no" far more than you would ever hear a "yes" come out of someone's mouth. I want to help change this. To me, goal setting should be done as often as you eat food; daily. This is going to keep you up to date with everything you need to get done. Additionally, it'll help you fill your time with more productive activities, rather than scrolling through Instagram until you find yourself on some persons account from Australia, who you must scroll back 12 times just to get to the main menu.

You have probably heard many times in your life the acronym of S.M.A.R.T Goals. Not to sound corny, but these are a smart thing to do.... No pity laughs please. I love the idea of setting goals, and I want you to love it too. As you live out your days, you might find that you don't have the drive to do some things that you may want to be doing.

Most of the people around us today think that once they have worked their 9-5 shift, that's it for the day. They don't need to keep doing anything for the rest of the day. This is the most fake thing you can tell yourself. It's easy to do this when you don't have anything else you want to get done during the rest of the day. Many people just fill the rest of their days with things that aren't furthering their life towards their dreams.

If you're already living your dream, then drop this book and forget everything I say because I can't tell you anything you don't already know. Stop wasting your time reading this and keep doing you.

If you aren't; keep reading and don't stop.

Goals are what's going to set you apart from you and the next-door neighbour that you hate, or your friend who's more successful than you. These goals are what's going to set you apart from everyone you know and want to be. To put it into a better perspective for you, do you think that someone who goes about their day without a care of what they are doing is going to make it to the same goal you want? No way. So why are you doing it? Stop wasting your day and set some goals that are going to put you on the right path.

It might be hard to set goals. You may think that you won't be able to reach those goals. They might seem to be impossible in the position that you are in right now. That's why you're looking at it all wrong, you're looking in the now. Goals are for the future. You could make them and then you're suddenly not in the same position that you were in the day before. Now you find yourself getting better every single day. Exactly why you need to be setting goals every day.

I want you to be better. The whole reason why I wrote this book was to help everyone who doesn't think that they can do something be the best that they possibly can. I have struggled with not reaching my full potential throughout most of my life. When I was in high school, I thought it was a great idea to never study before exams and not really do much homework. Obviously, that's just high school, and you're probably just thinking to yourself that it doesn't really matter. Except this set a bar for myself mentally, and it made it hard to get over it when it came to things outside of school. I couldn't see any reason to practice extra in sports or try harder in anything I really liked because I spent eight hours of my day not caring about something. Now, what I'm trying to get at here is to say that, my mistakes were my mistakes, and like I said before in the reason for this book, is to help you either avoid mistakes like mine or realize that you are making the same mistakes and that you need to make a change. Now, back to the book.

When the greatest people on the planet say, "Anyone can be anything they want to be," it's true. Now, you're probably saying in your head all the things that can hold you back, like your parents not caring what you do, friends that are bad influences that bring you down, an unsupportive group of people around you, no money, no schooling, etc. Well, what I have to say to that is… absolutely nothing. The world couldn't care less about what has happened to you or what continues to happen. A fun fact is that if you have problems, there is a good chance that your neighbours and your friends do. Even the billionaire that you want to be has problems. The question is, are these going to define you or are you going to go out there and allow yourself to achieve everything you want? Because you know that those don't hold you back. That is the meaning of "Anyone can do anything," it is a mindset.

The great thing is that as you get better and better at whatever it is you're doing, you realize just how much easier things are getting. It's easy to wake up early and start your day, you can spend more time on things you actually want to do, and you're not scared anymore. Goals can do this. Simply writing things down on a $20 whiteboard you buy at the dollar store can change how you live your life. This is one of the truest things I hope you take away from this.

I cannot stress the idea enough, that for you to start your life in the right direction, you must be willing to set goals. I want you to write down three things you want to achieve this week. I don't care what it is but write it down where you can see it. It can be "mow the lawn," "clean my room," or even "watch Gary Vee on YouTube." I don't care, just do it. If you want to increase your productivity and work towards what you actually want to do in life, set some goals. Start being the person you really want to be.

Questions:

What have I always wanted to do?

Where do I see myself in the next year? 5 Years? 10 Years?

Are you willing to write down a goal every morning?

Write down 3 goals you have for this week

1.
2.
3.

3

Don't Listen to Others

I'm going to be brutally honest here. This is very tough in today's new world of social media and the excess amount of internet that we are exposed to. We all love to have our followers "like" our pictures, and we all hate when they don't get enough of them. I would bet that more than 80% of the people that read this book use social media every day. Currently, as I write this book, I barely use my social media and only use them to promote my own podcast, "DIY Hustle".

For this chapter, I could easily go on about all that stuff, and it may help, but I don't feel that it would be as effective. Here are some tips for not giving a shit about what people around you think:

- Don't take what people say as the end all, be all.
- Stop using what your friends say as how you live your life.
- When you find what you love, be committed to it.

- Don't listen to jealous family/friends that try to bring you down.

Now I want to go through each one of these in detail so here you go.

DON'T TAKE WHAT PEOPLE SAY AS THE END ALL, BE ALL

Why does someone saying that you're stupid, make you think you're stupid? Why do you care so much? Why would you even consider that this person is right? Simply put, don't care what people say. You have to stick with yourself because you can't be jealous of yourself, but others can be. Everyone is vicious nowadays. What does that mean? Well it means that we all have access to some sort of technology, and with that we don't need to worry about the person on the other end of the screen. It's very easy now for someone to start talking shit about people without ever seeing that person in real life. That's not okay and can be very easy to bring your ideas down and make you less motivated. With the fact that we don't have to be around a person face to face anymore to talk, it's easy to say stuff that we don't actually mean or take the time to think about. You have to realize that other people won't know what the end looks like because they aren't on the same path as you are.

STOP USING WHAT YOUR FRIENDS SAY AS HOW YOU LIVE YOUR LIFE

It is true that we are the average of the five people we spend the most time with. You have most likely heard that already from someone you know or some other outlet. Your friends can be very influential to you, especially at a younger age. We all want to fit in, but does it make any sense to play along with want they think is best for you when you don't truly agree? You could be saying no to that, but you've probably done it in the past. We all have, so don't worry. This is about changing your future and making sure that you are doing what you want to be doing. Stop listening to what others think is the best for you and listen to your own heart.

WHEN YOU FIND WHAT YOU LOVE, BE COMMITTED TO IT

I cannot stress this point enough for you. Your life is about what you love and what makes you the happiest you can be. It's not about what others think is the best. I want you to know that whatever you love doing, it's worth doing, and you can figure it out along the way. There are people that get paid money to travel the world. Would you have ever thought that it was possible before someone went out and did it? This is because they loved to do it and stayed with it, and then the money came in later.

DON'T LISTEN TO JEALOUS FAMILY/FRIENDS THAT TRY TO BRING YOU DOWN

Oh, Taylor don't give me some point about haters. Sorry guys, but that's what I am about to do. I feel that in today's age, we think too much about what people say. You may see a couple comments or some negative feedback about something and take it as if they just tore you apart. They don't matter. People will continue to hate on successful people because they wish they were them. Everyone does it at every level and you need to learn to drown it out. They should become the fuel to your fire that keeps driving you to do the things you do. Show them just how great you really are and prove them wrong. Continue to shove success in their face and never let them win.

Questions:

What are the 4 tips the author lays out in this chapter?

1.
2.
3.
4.

Describe a time that you listened to what someone had to say, and then did that instead of what you actually wanted to do?

What do you love to do in your spare time?

How do you think you could make money off of it, really think about it?

4

Have More Than One Job

This is something I believe everyone should experience. Unless your first job is where you exactly want to be, then this does not apply. As for you, get more than one job; try new things out. I'm not saying you should work random jobs. I'm saying that experiencing more than one type of career path is a great way to see what you like and don't like.

Personally, by the time I was 20, I had seven jobs. All in different sectors. I worked in labour and restaurant jobs, as lot boy at a car dealership, and most recently, as a fitness centre receptionist What I found from doing these jobs is that I can't handle a shift job. I always need something to do. I'm sure that's just the entrepreneur in me though.

How our grandparents, and parents did the whole "job" thing is not the case for this generation. The article "Millennials in Search of a Different Kind of Career" by Gillian B. White published on June

12th, 2015 by The Atlantic[1] talks about how millennials differ from baby boomers when it comes to careers. They asked baby boomers what they thought of when it came to a job, and they said they thought about the money and to support the family. This differs from what millennials think of careers and what they do for their life; they want to make money, but doing that by having a career they are very interested in. That explains the growth of freelancing, and more and more people below the age of 35 are spending less time at one job.

Nowadays, we are more likely to run through about 15 or more jobs in our lifetime[2] (I've hit about half of that before 21). That's crazy to think about, but we're also a crazy generation. We don't know exactly what we want, but when we do find something, social media tells us differently. Learning that anything is possible makes figuring out what we want to do that much harder.

What can you do to start this? If you are in a job you hate, quit it. Enough said. I think that's the smartest thing you can do. If you work that job, you're keeping yourself from being happy. Look at it this way; if you are in a relationship that you hate or if you can't stand the other person, do you stay in it? No, you get the hell out of it. If you aren't in the position to quit that job, then start looking for a new job that is more based around what you like to do. If you like to go to the gym, apply to the gym you currently go to. If you like to talk to people and help them with their problems, get a sales job. Trying something new when it comes to a job can be such a rewarding experience and could possibly change your life.

On John Lee Dumas' Podcast *Entrepreneurs on Fire*, episode 1949 he has Chris Ducker on the show. Chris is an amazing person, and when you get time, I highly suggest listening to this great episode. He goes on to talk about how in today's world, we can do anything. Even publishing a book without a publisher and still getting it to be

---

[1] https://www.theatlantic.com/business/archive/2015/06/millennials-job-search-career-boomers/395663/

[2] https://www.edsurge.com/news/2017-07-20-how-many-times-will-people-change-jobs-the-myth-of-the-endlessly-job-hopping-millennial

a bestseller — which I am trying to do myself with this book. He goes on to say how we spend an average 50% of our day at work, and why you should want to be spending that doing something that you are excited about and love to do. Half of your day is a lot of time to be doing something you hate doing and not actually doing what you want. That's why spending time doing what you love doing and are excited about is so much more fulfilling even if you aren't making any money, (side hustle it if you need to get the bills paid for. Don't forget that you need something above your head but still need to work on your passion). Get away from that job you hate and find what you love. You'll find yourself feeling more fulfilled and better about life if you take the leap.

As I write this write this book, I can honestly say that from working the amount of jobs that I have, I've gained irreplaceable experience. I've also met so many amazing people throughout my life. Due to this, my network only expanded, which created even more opportunity for me to do anything I wanted.

I challenge you to start looking for a career that better fits you, and to do whatever it takes to get that career.

P.S., A career isn't a job. A job is something you do because you need money; a career is something you've decided to do for your whole life. At least in my eyes that is. I hope one day you never answer the question of "What do you do for a living?" with "Well my job is...," I want you to say, "I'm doing what I love".

Questions:

What don't you like about your job? Be as honest as possible.

Is there a job doing what you like? If not, can you create one?

List some things you can do to get a new job

1.
2.
3.

5

Don't Buy Stupid Stuff

This might possibly be the hardest chapter for some of you to read. We typically buy things that are obviously not necessary to survive. I'm not saying that this is a bad thing, we all do this, and we can thank marketing for that. Marketing is a big thing, and I'll touch on that later in the chapter. Back to buying stupid stuff. We all buy things, whether it be a new iPhone or those new shoes you bought even though you already have 10 others. The question is, are you in the position to buy all of this? If your bank account is dropping by a percentage of 1% when you make that purchase, it isn't a smart one (Made up percentage, but you get the point).

Now, this excludes groceries and other necessities of life. Getting that new Gucci or Yeezy's are far from it. You need to decide what your wants and needs are and separate what you're buying with those aspects. For example, if your mom or dad are super wealthy and you're using the money that they graciously give you to buy things that don't add legitimate value to your life, then you're doing something wrong. Start investing that money, and when I say that, I don't just mean in stocks or business ventures, but in yourself. Buy some books or buy tickets to an event where you're going to learn new things. Maybe even start buying and selling products with that money. I have friends that had money to do these things but never thought about it. I find that incredibly stupid.

For those that don't have money handed to them and instead must work hard for it; don't waste it. You work hard, so make sure that money isn't going to be spent somewhere that isn't giving you the same value back. Excuse me now for using the word "value" many times throughout this chapter.

One thing you should always do before you make a purchase, is ask yourself "is this a want, or do I absolutely need this to survive?". From this you can tell whether there is a value gained from that product. The people who are always adding value to the life that they live are going to be more successful.

Now, I know this chapter is easy to dispute and maybe you're reading it thinking that all of this is total garbage. I honestly think that the people who look at this concept and take something from this and possibly, just once, stop and think about what purchases they are making, will be instantly more successful.

I want you to take five minutes to write out everything you have bought in the past two weeks. After you have done this, separate them by "wants" and "needs". Take the prices of the "wants" and multiply it by 26 (number comes from you buying these "wants" on a bi-weekly average because of pay days). That is most likely the average of how much of your hard-earned money you have wasted on things that aren't bringing you back sufficient value. I want you to be keeping that for yourself. The first step to this is already completed. You now see how much money you waste. The second step is to take 2-3 things off that list, not spend money on those things, and redirect that money to valued items. Some of these items may be books. A workout program, better food, or whatever brings greater value to what you want to do with your life.

Eric Thomas, a popular motivational speaker that lived homeless in the streets of Detroit for 2 years of his life, has a great line that I still think of and love to this very day. He says, "You can burn my house down, but if you took away what's in my head, then I will have truly lost everything". Do you understand that? It doesn't matter how many things you get in your life. If you haven't learned things and put your knowledge into obtaining more knowledge, you are always going to be vulnerable to the things you don't know. Eric can always get another house if he knows how to get a million dollars. He has spent the time and allocated his money into learning what he needs to do to obtain his goals and what to do to be financially free. Why are you doing exactly the opposite? You're putting yourself into a vulnerable position by wasting the money you're earning instead of focusing on what you could be spending on to gain more money.

Understanding the concept of not spending your money on dumb stuff is so crucial to becoming the person you want to become. This is becoming very hard to do because of social media and how marketing takes place nowadays. Influencer marketing has become so dominant for companies to advertise their products on due to its high visibility. You are more likely to buy an item that you see your favourite influencer using just because you like them. You feel personally connected with that person and don't see a problem buying the product, yet it wasn't really your decision. Is that okay with you? Is that how you want to live your life? Marketing is how the world goes around…partly. It is how products get noticed and there's nothing wrong with that, but you shouldn't be allowing this to make your decisions.

Now, this isn't about you spending less and saving more. I would argue that you should be spending the same amount of money. You need to start spending your money on things that help you become better than you are now. Those items are up to you. A long time ago,

I chose to make sure that the money I spend is going to help me along my path, and instead isn't being wasted or used for things that can't do that. Now, it's your turn. Looking at yourself is a big part of this as you'll see in many of the following chapters.

Questions:

What products do you know that you over spend on?

Why do you spend money on these items?

What tips were provided to spend less on these items?

What is the definition of stupid stuff?

6

Be Wrong

Being wrong can be the best thing ever, depending on how you look at it. How I look at being wrong is that now I have had the opportunity to learn something new and avoid making that mistake again. Looking at this gives us the chance to become even better people. Being wrong can be the best thing ever.

Most people are afraid to be wrong and in turn, they are wrong. Why are you fearing something that is going to only make you better? Making a mistake is a part of everyone's life. No one can just spend every day doing all things the right way, it's simply impossible. If you think Warren Buffett has never made a bad investment before, you're wrong. What he did was he took the information that he gained from putting his money into a bad investment and then made sure to keep that in mind when he went to invest in other things. This man is one of the richest people on the planet and he has been wrong many times. Do you think that maybe you should be to?

I'm not saying that you should be seeking out this factor. I'm saying that it is okay to take a risk and be wrong then it is to never take the steps to get there. If you just want to play it safe and always want to be right, then you're never going to be the best at whatever you are doing. Playing it safe may be a popular belief to be getting the best out of any situation, but this really isn't the case. The more you play it safe the more you are just holding yourself back from being great. As you keep holding yourself back, opportunities that you would have been able to get aren't there since you never truly threw yourself at what you were doing. I don't see why anyone that wants to be successful would ever do this, it just doesn't make sense to me.

From my experience, being in lectures and attending British Columbia Institute of Technology (BCIT), I noticed that even if the professor asked the simplest question, no one would put up their hand to answer even though we all knew what the answer to it was. The reason why no one wants to answer it was because we were all afraid to not be right and look stupid for trying. The only reason why you would look stupid, is because we didn't answer the question. How can the professor ask such an easy question, and no one answer it? We don't look stupid for trying; we looked stupid for not trying. The more time you spend trying to avoid making the mistake instead of putting up your hand and taking the chance to be correct instead of just sitting there, the more time you're going to spend working towards success. Now even if you were to answer the question and not be correct, wouldn't that be a good thing? You have now made sure that the way you thought was either correct or incorrect. Since you now have confirmed you were not correct in your thinking, for the future you will always be correct. That is the power of being wrong.

I'm not in school, Taylor. That doesn't make sense for me, Taylor. Okay, and this is what I have to say. That's bullshit. What about when you don't say something to your girlfriend or boyfriend about something they were asking you. Or even before you are in a relationship and that girl or boy you have a total crush on says something or makes a move on you, but you're not sure, and you just sit there and don't do anything about it because you're afraid of reading the signs wrong. Well guess what? You'll never know in that moment unless you do something. Why hear from your friends later something that you could have known in that moment?

This also leads into fight or flight or even freeze modes that we all possess. If you don't know what that is, it is time in which you either decide to run away from something, or face it head on. I would hope you take the latter. Flight in this situation would be to not ask a question, or to not answer a question. Whereas being in fight mode, you would be engaged in the conversation and asking questions and attempting to answer any that come your way as well. Although fight mode does sound like you're getting more done and being more productive, if you aren't making sure that your actions are productive instead of just asking a ton of questions for no reason, then you're screwed. The person who is asking and answering questions is typically going to be one of the more successful people in the room because of this attitude, which is going to be a part of their life. If you let this attitude consume you and you are always looking for knowledge, then you've learned what this chapter is all about. The more time you spend trying to learn and know more about your respected field, the more time you'll be working towards being successful. I'm sure you want that. Never freeze up. Don't find yourself not having the words or never being able to take any action at all. It would be better to run away and learn from that then it would be to stop and know you're supposed to go and be a little bitch. Each of these can have their own pros and cons. You just need to be able to use each one in the right situation. Sometimes it may be good to catch your tongue because you shouldn't be speaking so quickly, and sometimes you should be holding your own.

With all this being said, you probably won't be able to just flip the switch and start being that person that is always asking questions. You must start with baby steps, making sure you ask one question for a couple of meetings is a great way to start this. As time progresses, make sure that you're asking more questions, or as soon as you're not clear on something, see what is going on with that. There is no harm in clarifying something. It will only hurt you if you decide not to ask a simple question. Other steps you could take could be

- Always be present, if you don't do this you won't know what's going on.
- Create questions throughout the day and ask them.
- Don't be afraid for the answer you "could" get, just as the damn question.

Being wrong is such a fulfilling thing to do. The valuable knowledge you can gain from doing such a thing is incredible. It's up to you to make sure that you're taking the right steps to assure you are doing this. I always think that if you're 20-30 years old, these are the prime years to be wrong at things. You have the time to correct these mistakes and may or may not have a family to support yet or have a super locked down job. Now, respect if you do have these things already, but if you want to continue to grow in these things, you'll have to decide.

With that being said, being non-reactive in certain situations is an asset as well. Being non- reactive can save you from a huge mistake because you listened to your head and how you felt instead of allowing your emotions to control you. That is something I will speak on in the next chapter.

Being indecisive will be the death of you. The time you spend having to choose between certain things and never making up your mind is going to eat up the most precious thing you have; your time. People like Grant Cardone and Gary Vaynerchuk both talk about how they have made up their mind in many cases. They are some of the masters of making up their minds and being certain in what they are doing. Indecisiveness stems from being uncertain in what you are doing. Steve Jobs could have spent time trying to think whether his business would end up being what it is now, but instead he was certain that it would. Some part of him just knew that it would, and that is what helped drive him.

Now, you're probably wondering what this has to do with being wrong. To be able to be certain about something, you're accepting the fact that you could be wrong, and doing it anyways. You don't spend your time wondering about things and then regretting it later. I want you to take a chance and allow yourself to be wrong about something and see how much you learn from it.

Questions

Why should you take a chance in being wrong?

What is the main reason why people don't want to ask questions?

What steps can you take in your life to ask more questions?

What are the 3 modes your body will take in certain situations and define them?

7

Develop Your EQ

If you want to read an entire book about this, you can get *Emotional Intelligence 2.0* by Travis Bradberry and Jean Greaves which contains a lot of tests and really takes this topic to the level I wish I could. Emotional Intelligence, in my opinion, is of far greater value then IQ. Being more emotionally stable and in-tune can help you handle situations in a more thoughtful way. Doing so will most likely get you that end goal you wanted. Now, that's just my opinion, but here are some scenarios that show you why EQ can have a bigger impact than IQ.

Let's say you're a salesperson at a phone provider. A customer comes in and is super outraged. The logic of what he says doesn't make sense and you know that. He's complaining about a bill that was 100% correct and was totally his fault for going over his data plan. Now, if you based this conversation on just your IQ, you would tell him the facts without really catering to the fact that he isn't in the best of moods. This would only further enrage him and escalate the situation at hand. This would most likely result in your manager having to come into the conversation and deal with it. Now, that isn't a good look for your manager, let alone you. If you had used your

EQ, then this situation would take an interesting turn. You would be able to provide great service, as well as be able to really understand where he is coming from. You would not just throw information or details at him that don't really matter unless you express some sort of empathy. This will only result in better situations for the both of you, and you would never have to deal with the awkward situation of getting your manager into the mix because you know exactly how to handle it.

This is a topic that a lot of people struggle with because most people don't want to cater to other people's feelings and their needs. To become successful at anything you want to do, you're going to have to really understand this topic. This information is in bite-sized form, and at the end of this chapter and book, you will see references to other books that dive more into this topic. There are books as well as classes on this topic. One that I will reference is Dale Carnegie's book, *How to Win Friends and Influence People,* which essentially is a textbook that he had written for his classes. What he mainly talks about is that you can't be all about the "Me" and how you really must understand what others want.

According to the dictionary, the definition of Emotional Intelligence is:

"The capacity to be aware of, control, and express one's emotions, and to handle interpersonal relationships judiciously and empathetically."

Now, why would you not want to practice this? Do you really want to go your whole life only thinking about yourself and what you want? Or do you look at this as an opportunity to further yourself in your career and all actions that you take each day?

Self-Awareness is a big part of being able to have more emotional intelligence. You can easily drive up your EQ just by becoming more self-aware. It isn't easy and requires a lot of real life practice and may involve you having to set goals in the process to make sure you're on the right path. I know what I am and who I am, but this has come from a lot of hard work and really understanding myself better. I asked myself these questions:

- Who am I?
- Who am I not?
- Why am I here?

These three simple questions helped me really take my mind and self to the next level. This helped me write this book that you're currently taking the time to read. It helped me start my podcast "DIY Hustle". Also, whatever else I am currently doing in the future after this book is released.

The time is now for you to start spending it on learning about who you really are. If you're reading this and don't really have anywhere in life you particularly want to go, ask yourself those questions. Start investing in yourself and thinking about what you really want to do. As soon as you do this, you will see yourself working a lot harder than ever before, and much happier.

Emotional Intelligence 2.0 is a great read and allows you to take the EQ test within it and start taking the steps to becoming more emotionally intelligent. That's the one thing that I love about this, you can easily think that having a better IQ is quite hard to achieve and you may never want to go for it, but having a better EQ isn't that hard. You just need to critique the way you currently think and you'll be on your way to bettering yourself.

Questions:

What does Emotional Intelligence mean to you?

What are to key aspects to EQ and how will you implement it into your life?

What are 3 questions you can ask yourself to start this process?

How can you be more self-aware?

8

Audit How You Talk and Think

How do you talk daily? How do you talk about your friends? Money? Life? School? Your parents? What do you think and say about these things? Something that most people don't do is look at how they speak. If you talk negatively, you're probably a negative person. The opposite is also true. If you are a positive person and speak in a "can-do" attitude, then that's they type of person you will be. Grant Cardone touches on this subject a bit in his book *The 10X Rule*.

He talks about how the most successful people have this undeniable can-do attitude. They don't look at something and think that it would be unattainable; they say to themselves and others that it is possible, and that they will achieve it. Average people like to overlook this and think that it doesn't matter how they talk. How they only want to a talk the same way they have their whole life. Let's face it, if you want to achieve the highest of success, then you're going to have to make a change.

It isn't easy to watch every single thing that you say in one day, I get that. You should be watching for when you tend to say something that isn't in a positive mindset. The more times you can catch yourself when you start saying things like "we can't do that" or "that isn't possible" or "no way", simply take a step back and say the word "can". The more times you say it, the less you think things to be impossible. In this decade we can see that more and more things are becoming possible, and that's true for everyone's life. With technology and everything else on this planet that's growing, we can honestly say that this is the generation of opportunity. You just need to change your "cant's" into "cans".

I see people close to me always telling me that becoming the person I want to be won't be possible or that it involves a lot of work. One time, I was pushed so much that I honestly thought myself that it wouldn't be possible. At that time, I realized that I wasn't telling myself the right things, and that I needed to make a change. Right at that moment, I made the change and listened to how I was talking to myself. This led to me changing how I ran my life and what I did on a daily basis. It practically created the person that is writing this book for you right now. What you can tell from that story is that I looked at home, I was talking to myself (auditing), and then made the decision to change it right away before it got the best of me. Now, the other part of this story is that the people around me were telling me that I would never be able to get to the point of my life that I wanted to be at. I changed that as well and made sure that I'd one day prove to them that I will be there. Doing so changed their approach to the same conversation forever.

What I want you to take away from that story is that as long as you take the small amount of time to do this, it will help extremely. The great part is that it's free for you to do. You don't need to pay some fee to audit your brain and how you talk. This is all on you to do yourself. If the top 1% do it, why don't you do it? This will help you in your work life, relationships, marriage, and family. It can help every aspect of your life.

The more positive you are, the more people gravitate towards you. Since they themselves can't be positive, they will look at you and see what they wish they could be. People don't want to be positive sometimes because they are scared to try and achieve new things. If you are always going out with the attitude and the intent of the "can-do" attitude, I guarantee that more people will gravitate towards you. You will find that your boss is more likely to give you that raise if you practice this. So many great things can come of this. If you continue to say it throughout anything you do, failure will never be an option.

You're probably thinking "What if I do this but don't get what I wanted?", well that would mean somewhere along the line you need to be able to accept defeat in some aspects of your life. You're not going to be great at everything. Do not allow yourself to get stuck in that way of thinking. The quicker you're able to accept defeat after you've worked your ass off in getting a new deal or getting that job you always wanted, the quicker you can become more accepting of your life and the things that are around you. These things may be aspects of your life that you can't even change, and that means you should not spend the time trying to or feeling sorry for yourself. Once you can point out the difference between what you can and can't change in your life, you can start to manifest a new you.

In the movie *Pursuit of Happiness,* in the scene where Will Smith and his son are at the basketball court playing around, Will's character tells his own son that he won't be able to do something. He immediately regrets it – realizing that he shouldn't be using the "can't" word around his son – and then proceeds to tell his son that he should never listen to anyone who tells him that he can't do something. This is in a move called the *Pursuit of Happiness,* people. How can that get any clearer? Take some time, write down negative things that you say in your normal day, and then remove them from your vocabulary. This is only going to better how you live your life.

Questions:

What are things that you say during the day that you hate?

Do you talk negative about yourself and/or others. If so, how can you stop this?

What are aspects of your life that you are able to change around you, list 3 of them? (i.e. friends)

-

-

-

9

Be You

You always need to stay true to what you want people to think of you. This generation always wants others to tell them what they should do and always listen. The less time you spend listening to what others say, the more successful you will become. With the growing use of social media and youth wanting "likes" and people to engage with them, it's easy to get caught up with other people's thoughts.

This is where you have it wrong. You need to spend less time thinking about how many likes you are getting and spend more time looking at what you are putting out there and how much value it is giving people. I have a podcast called DIY Hustle. I get an average of 40 listens on SoundCloud each episode. I don't care about this at all, I only care that I am putting out content that is giving those 40-people value. Simply put, that's the difference. The less time you spend looking for likes, the more you will get. It sounds contradictory but it's true.

Gary Vaynerchuk talks about this a lot. He has an episode that is directed towards 20-year old's and goes over this topic a bit. The episode is titled "Advice for every 20-year-old,"and it currently sits as one of his most viewed YouTube videos, and by my standards holds the most useful information by far. This was a big inspiration for this book and helped me turn my own life around.

He gets a call from a woman named Taylor and she has a problem with trying to make sure that she is doing enough with her life. She currently is 22 years old and just got out of college. They talk about a lot, but I want to focus on one comment she makes about looking at the Kardashians and what they are doing and how Kylie Jenner has created a business when she is 19 years old and make $500 million in a year already. Gary makes the obvious point that this family is uber rich already and that Kris Jenner is an amazing business woman. What she is doing wrong is comparing herself to this family. That isn't who she is nor, will it be if she continues to do so. If she spends more time working on who she is and doing what she can to get great at what she does, that is what will help her in her life. Looking at Instagram famous people or anyone that is giving the appearance of being rich on these platforms isn't worth comparing yourself to. The more time you spend looking at Kylie Jenner, Hawk Reece, Jake Paul, or anyone else that has these amazing lives, you're just going to hold yourself back.

It's very easy to get into a habit of doing this though. You probably follow their accounts, so they show up on your feeds all the time. Now, this is the point that I would tell you to unfollow them and start working on the only person worth following; yourself. I would even go as far as to say that you should just shut down your social media accounts (provided you don't use them for your business).

If you could spend time being the one posting content instead of looking at that content, that is the point you should be trying to get to. People that have amassed these huge followings and generated so much for themselves, but don't really spend much time on social media. They spend the time on social media to learn and see how they can tailor the accounts they have to make even better content and attraction.

Gary Vaynerchuk has people that post most of his content for him because he's such a busy person – although he does post a lot himself, since having your own personal aspect is huge. Having a personal brand will set you apart from others around you. If you create a brand where all you do is hard work and get down to it, then people will know you for that, and when they think of a hard worker, they will think of you. Check out some of your favourite influencers and see what their brand may be.

Looking at all that I hope you can see why you shouldn't be spending time looking at others and comparing it to yourself, as well as having others make your decisions for you. Why are you spending the most valuable thing you have on other people? Time is the only thing you can't get more of, and these people who you don't even know are eating it up.

In an interview by Gerard Adams on Leaders Create Leaders, he interviews Chris Stoikos. He is the founder of Dollar Beard Club which he took from a company worth $0 to a $24 million company. He touches on the fact that people are always doing things that they don't want to do, whether it be an appointment they don't want to go to or a job they hate. He puts it plain and simple and just how I love it, "If you don't want to do something, don't do it, that's not you, be you".

Everyone has those times when they don't want to do something, but they still end up doing it and have a crappy time whilst doing it. Does having a crappy time sound like fun? So why are you not just filling your time with things that you would want to be doing and are excited to be doing?

I spend my whole day making sure that I am not doing things that are unnecessary. If I don't want to be talking with someone, I go do something else. If I don't want to work at a job, then I quit and find a job I would rather be doing. I have done these many times. As I talked about in *More than One Job* I have had seven jobs in the past 4-5 years. Each time I knew I disliked what I was doing, so I looked for something else, so I wasn't just wasting my time at a place that I knew I would never want to move up in or spend 16 hours a day doing. I made sure that I was being myself and that I was always being happy doing what I wanted to be doing. These changes of jobs came with a lot of jokes made at me and demeaning comments. My own family making jokes that I've had so many jobs, and others saying that it was "weird" that I don't stay with one job. I found it weird that they were spending the most valuable thing they had at a place that wasn't making them happy.

As Chris says in his interview, "Be You". I hope that sticks with you. Amid all the pressure from other people, you need to stay true to yourself and what you decide you want to be. Don't let things like social media, your friends, family, and even your teachers tell you what you are. Being you is the largest asset you can have. If you know who you are and stick with it through the worst times, when you get to the good times, things will just flow. If you want to be happy all the time and be on that "Vocation" - whatever that is - we are told about when we were kids, then this is for you. If you're comfortable being the product of what others want you to be, disregard what I just said and give this book to someone else who wants this.

Questions:

Who do you admire?

What makes you different from them?

Why is being yourself beneficial to you?

What will you do to make sure that you are always being yourself and not being another person?

10

Find Someone Doing What You Want to Do

You may find that this contradicts what I said in the earlier chapter about being yourself. What I want you to take away from this is that you need to find that person who is doing what you would like to do, but still shape it for yourself. This is a great way to shape yourself in the beginning, but you still must take the efforts later on to stay true to yourself.

The point is simple. If you want to be a marketer, look at Gary. If you want to get into sales and be good at it, read up on Grant Cardone. The same goes for every other respective field. If you want to be great at basketball, watch videos on how Lebron James and Stephen Curry play. That's something so obvious, yet few people do this. You need to see what the best person is doing in whatever you're doing and see what they do in a usual day. Do they wake up at 6am and work till 12pm? If so, then why are you not doing that? If you're getting up at 8am and working until 6pm, you're never going to catch up to what they are. Everyone has the same amount of time in the day, so why aren't you using it as effectively as that person is? There's no reason for you not to be taking full advantage of the life that you have been given.

As you spend your time looking at what they are doing and start to mirror some of those things, you will eventually get to the point that you won't need to do so anymore. Instead, you will be the person that others need to mirror. That, I think, is one of the greatest achievements along your journey. If you can be a role model for future generations, or even for your children. That is a great achievement no matter what and should never be looked down on as not good enough.

Throughout my life, I've found that I want to follow people who have the same drive that I have. Currently, I would have no problem working for someone who has a successful business doing what I want to do. The kicker about this is that I would easily do it for free. The point of this is that I realize that the knowledge that I would gain from this time with that person — whoever that may be — is worth much more in the long run.

What most people think is that they can just become the best at something by just learning from a book or in a classroom. That is only going to carry you so far. Taking advantage of learning from the best or following someone who has what you want and doing the same things, is going to take that to another level. The more time you spend being around what you want to do, (1) You will be much happier, (2) By being exposed to that job and seeing how people do it at the highest level, you will learn as well. Everyone can work at a normal level, that's why it is called normal. Do you really want to be just like everyone else and live your life that way? Or would you rather be the only person who could do what you do because you have gotten so great at it that no one else compares? I would hope it is the latter.

Look at Amazon, they are the one stop shop for pretty much everything you want, and on top of that, it can be at your house in as little as one day. They aren't just stopping with this; they are looking to be the first delivery service that has someone come into your house instead of leaving it at the door, like how it's been done for years. They are simply becoming the best at what they do, and that is why Jeff Bezos is being recognized as such a brilliant man.

I watch a lot of Gary Vaynerchuk; I'm going to be honest. What I picked up from watching him was the habit of going to sleep at Midnight and waking up around 6am every day. This allows me to get up in the morning, go to the gym, and get started on my day before everyone else is even awake. I looked at someone who is doing exactly what I want to do and started picking up things that he has talked about. This has created a new life for me, and I instantly saw more things getting done in my life. I was never behind in anything because I was adding 2 hours each day to my life. This all adds up as well. If you're usually waking up at 8am every day and going to sleep at 10pm, I am getting about 1,344 more hours of work in each year that you aren't. I find that extremely useful because in those hours I am finding more ways to become successful and reaching my goals that I have for myself.

Now you don't need to wake up earlier to get better. You can simply look at what you're doing each day and cut out the bullshit that's in there (typically social media scrolling and pointless YouTube videos). Spend more time looking at who you want to be and start picking up things that they do. Spend some time right now researching what you love to do and find that person that is at the top of it. Then find out what they have done to get there and pick up some good habits. You will see some things changing in your life, most likely for the better.

Questions:

Who are you watching that is doing what you love to do?

What makes them so interesting to you and why you would want to watch them?

Can you do this job? (Answer is most likely a yes)

Why would you not be able to do this? (Leave blank)

11

Always Love Rejection

Weird, right? Why would I want to love rejection when that is purposefully putting me into a position of feeling like shit? Well, that's the point. The more times you are put in the position of being wrong or rejected, you become better. If you're wrong, get over it, and then go out and never make that mistake again. Do not take a mistake as an excuse to give up. That is how most people see things nowadays. They make one mistake and someone either makes fun of them for it or gets mad at them, and they immediately give up and never try again. That is so sad to see because that wasn't a reason to just give up. I hate when I have a conversation with someone I know, and they talk about how they aren't doing something anymore because they didn't feel they could do it or they didn't get the results they wanted right away. I always ask them "Why didn't you stick with it?" And they usually say some sort excuse that is about whether they didn't have time, or something went wrong with it. I am always left thinking to myself that if they had just stuck with it and pushed through they would have made something of it. Don't expect quick results.

If you spend time listening to the most influential people on the planet, they all at one point were rejected from something they were doing. For example, you probably know someone named Oprah Winfrey. If you haven't listened to her story, then this will probably be very surprising to you. She was fired from an anchor job. Oprah Winfrey is by far one of the most successful people on the planet and has made quite the name for herself. Although this is true, she too experienced rejection. She didn't just quit thought, she kept pursuing her dream and didn't stop when people told her she wasn't good at being in front of a camera. Like I said before, the less time you focus on what the negatives about a situation are, the more successful you'll be. Look to just keep grinding and working hard. You'll get to where you want to be, it just takes time and a lot of work.

Learning to love this is going to be tough at the start. The best job to work to get a real handle on this is door to door sales. I have a friend who works this type of job. He co-runs the podcast with me. On a typical day, he would go to about 40-50 doors. He makes about 1-2 sales a day — now that's on average — and loves it. He gets doors slammed in his face, told to get off people's properties, and basically gets a "fuck you" every day. I think that is amazing. He can go a whole day through this and keep going every day for over a year now. He even takes an extra shift each week. With that being said, the man gets rejected a lot, but he doesn't just give up. He has learned that not everyone is going to just say "yes" and that sometimes it's going to happen. It doesn't have to affect his day or work. He's learned that rejection is a part of life and to take it with a grain of salt. Being rejected like that can help you in so many ways, and here's a few:

- Less fear of the unknown
- Can ask that girl, or boy you've always wanted to ask out with confidence

- Knowing what you're doing wrong in your job and what to fix
- Always being able to be yourself without fear

You're probably wondering why you would be able to be yourself because you have gone through rejection, but that's pretty much it. The more times you get rejected for whatever you are doing, the more you will hopefully start to think about what you're doing and realize it isn't you, it's just how life is. This in turn will allow you to always be yourself and never have to be fake in anything that you do. I think that everyone should be themselves (See Tip 9) and never be allowing themselves to be molded by someone else.

A friend of mine goes through so much rejection at his current job and I think that it's really helped him to understand how he wants to approach every new door he goes up to. In the future, I expect him to be able to do everything without having to worry about what that person is going to say. He has gone through this rigorous training already. I applaud him for being able to always get up and go to the next door without worrying about what is going to happen, because if it is going to happen he is the reason why. In a full commission job like that, no one can get you your money except for yourself. It's not his bosses fault, the owners fault, the customers fault; it's his own fault. To be able to understand that is a powerful thing. To not blame others for our own short comings is going to be one of your strongest assets in life.

Now, you don't have to work a door to door job to understand and experience this. You just need to simply start asking more questions at your workplace and start speaking your mind more. Understanding that the worst that can happen is you get rejected, which is great. Everyone will experience it; we are all going to go through it. What really matters is that you don't take things as a personal attack against your ego (see next chapter). I believe that you can start living your life how you want to when you love being rejected.

Questions:

Will you blame others for your own actions, why not?

Why is rejection such a powerful thing?

How can rejection help you in your life?

Where can you put yourself in a position to be rejected?

12

Kick the Ego

Having an ego is simply a waste of time. The time spent believing that you are so much better than other people and shouldn't listen or care for what they are saying is a waste. You probably have an ego right now, whether you don't like people correcting you when you're wrong, or when they correct your grammar. It could even be that someone complains about your work or how you do your work. A great example would be if you're in school and you have a project you are doing with a partner. Let's say that your partner isn't your friend this time around, and you have been matched up with someone you don't like. To begin the project, he/she complains to you that you're doing something wrong and this absolutely infuriates you. You already want to go to the teacher and tell them you can't work together and that you're going to end up with the worst grade you've ever gotten. Obviously, the teacher doesn't want to deal with your nonsense and says you will have to deal with it and work together because the groups have already been made and changes just simply aren't possible.

You can make two choices at this point. You can make the decision to keep complaining and get into useless spats throughout your project and never get the work done that you want to. Or you could spend time understanding what the person has problems with and make the decision to understand and not take their comments to heart, which would cloud in your judgement. I would recommend the latter, not only do you get your work done, but you might create a friendship out of it. One that could be very long-lasting, which you never knew could happen.

A point that I always look at as well is when Gary Vaynerchuk talks about never expecting anything from anyone. He never thinks to be getting something back because he knows that it isn't going to change his world if he isn't to get it back. He doesn't think of himself as a super human that deserves rewards for things that he has done in the past. He overlooks that, and from the very beginning, when he helps someone he doesn't look at the future of him receiving some sort of monetary value back to him. This is something a lot of us don't do. We always want to receive something in return for what we have done in the past. When you work harder at your job, you instantly start thinking you should receive a raise, and when they don't give it to you right away, you stop working as hard. Did you ever think that if you worked harder without expecting that raise, maybe it would have come a lot quicker because you didn't talk about it so much with your coworkers or complain about it when you had to stay an extra hour after work? The less time you had spent doing that and put that into your work, the more likely you could have gotten to that raise. If you kicked that ego to the side and just put your head down and worked, this would have happened at some point.

This can also lead to you blaming your boss, the company, your friend that wants you to go out every weekend, or your wife for always wanting to have dinner at 6 when you could have stayed at work. Do you ever see in there the word "Yourself"? You need to stop blaming others. This is where your ego kicks in and where you believe you're the best and nothing should be your fault. I beg to differ. Everything should be YOUR fault. It's your fault if the work doesn't get done, your fault for leaving work early, your fault that you didn't get the raise you wanted, and your fault that you went out on the weekend. I never hear people look at themselves and think about what they could have done differently and always see them blame other people. That doesn't make sense. It's your life, right? Why are you trying to make it seem like these other factors make up who you are and what you do. They don't because you made these decisions, and if you didn't have that dreaded ego, you would see it.

You need to stop blaming others and understand that it isn't anyone else's fault but your own. Everything that happens in your life is based off what you allow to happen. Not your mothers fault, your fathers fault, your high school teachers fault; it's all on you. When you understand that things just get way better and life is on a different level.

In "How to Win Friends and Influence People" by Dale Carnegie, he talks about how other people matter much more then you do. He mainly talks about how to understand that other people are who matter on this planet because nothing will get done if you want to do it all by yourself. Who is supposed to buy your product? Other people. Who are the investors? Other people. Who understands what you don't have time to understand because you need the time to focus on the parts that you need to focus on in your life? Other people. So why do you need to have an ego that puts others down or not trust another person to help you get something done? That just won't help you in the long run. You will just bring yourself down. If you want to be as successful as you can be, you need to get rid of that fucking ego and treat everyone as if they are going to get you a million dollars tomorrow, because everyone on this planet is worth something and should never be treated like you are way better than them. Be grateful and never expect something from someone because that could be when you get the most from them.

Questions:

Do you see the need to have an ego?

Has your ego gotten in the way of doing the right thing?

Can you get around having an ego and live a better life because of it?

13

Practice Patience

I get it, you already want everything to be right in front of you. You want that big house or super luxurious car. You don't see yourself taking less than a year to make a million dollars. I know what that feels like, because I have done it in the past. I quickly realized when I started up my business that it is going to be a grind, and I didn't expect to be making any money at all. In fact, I did the job for free for the first client I brought on. The market will show you how hard it is to grow a business and that will be the real test for you.

A great story of someone who took a while to get to where they are now, is Ryan Serhant. He is currently 10 years into the Real Estate game over in New York City, one of the greatest places I have visited in my life because of the feeling you get when you stand in Times Square. This obviously was no easy task to get to where he is now. He is on the show "Million Dollar Listings," the original show that allowed him to grow his personal brand. This wasn't until after he went through a ton of shitty times. He didn't just start to sell these amazing places. He started at the bottom just like everyone else. He soon grew to who he is now, but that was after working every single day and not normal hours like everyone else. Obviously not everyone has the same drive as he did, but that is the whole point of this book and what I am trying to help you understand.

To get the maximum out of your life, you need to be passionate about what you're doing so you can work as much or as little as you want to on it.

Let's do some of the math here. Say you are being patient enough to get to your goal and expect something to happen in 10 years. On a daily average, you're working 15 hours a day on it because you love it. That's a total of 5,475 hours a year, and a total of 54,750 hours in that 10-year span. If you're working a normal 8-hour day on it and every day of the year, that's only 2,920 hours, and 29,200 in those 10 years. For that person to get to where you are they need to work for another 9 years almost. This is because you decided to be work patiently because it'll pay off in the end.

If you think that it is going to be super hard to get to where you want, and you don't want it to be like that, you must face the facts. It's going to be a grind. You're going to make mistakes along the way that may be hard to overcome. This is all true, but in the end, you're still always doing what you love to do, and you'll want to get up every morning to grind at it. This is something a lot of entrepreneurs struggle with, as well as most people that have a career. As well us millennials, since we love things handed to us — sorry everyone reading this, but it's true — and we don't think about that a lot. Some of us (big ups to everyone who hasn't had everything handed to them and have fought their way through it, respect) have had many things we have either bought for us or made easy to get. Frankly, the real world isn't really like that. This is where if you have the patience to get what you want, it will work out quite better.

YouTube took forever to blow up (in millennial time that is). If you were on it when it first started, you probably still aren't on it because the interest just wasn't there. YouTube started getting more popular in 2009 and started building up to where it really got interesting in 2012-2013. Now, when I said that it started getting popular in 2009, anyone could have started a vlog or a cosmetic page, and it would most likely have been the first or have been one of the few. Now there are tons of these pages and people can survive fully just off making content for YouTube. Most of these people have been on it for the long term and built these channels into what they are today. That's some real patience.

Don't expect shit to be handed to you. That's all I want you to know. I also understand that myself, as I am only 20 years old. The thing that I know is that it's going to take a long time for me to get to where I want to be, and I am not trying to rush myself there. I am content with knowing that the work I put in now will get me to where I want to be, and the little victories that I have along the way are reassuring me that this is the right way to be thinking. The time you spend rushing what you are doing or try to take shortcuts will only hold yourself back. Do you understand that? Instead of spending time running around a problem, face it head on (i.e. not taking that shortcut). This will only mean better for you because either 1. You now don't have that problem ever come up again 2. You've learned a valuable lesson from that problem that now has led to you being able to fix other problems. Get it now? Have some patience and you won't feel rushed in what you are doing. That way, you won't need to find shortcuts anymore. I plead this to you, I want you to know about this idea because it will help. I know as millennials, we want things quick and more likely easy. That isn't going to help you. I've had my problems with these aspects of myself and have learned that it just isn't possible to work if you want to be big time or even just an effective employee at your work. Start to take things slower, accept those problems you need to overcome, and take them head on. It may take an extra hour of your day, or an extra day, but it will feel a lot better later on. Patience is everything, nothing is just handed to you because you want it quickly.

"I'm a tortoise in a hare's costume"
– Gary Vaynerchuk

Questions:

Are you in the position to be patient with things you want in your life?

How can being more patient help your life?

14

Don't Waste Time

One thing I hear a lot from my classmates or my friends is that they don't have time to do certain things. They don't have time to attempt a new business idea, go to the gym, meet for coffee to talk because they have homework. I hear this all the time, and quite frankly I'm tired of it. One thing I want you to do is ask yourself how you fill your time. Do you spend your time on social media looking at memes on 9gag? Or do you spend it trying to network and message potential clients? There is a huge difference in how you spend your time and how much it will affect whether you are getting something done in your day.

If you think about the amount of time you spend doing dumb shit, it's quite significant. I used to find myself sitting on Instagram looking at pictures and videos for five minutes, and then 10, and before I knew it, it turned into 30 minutes. That was time that I could have been using to either read a book, apply something that I wanted to for the past little while, or even just get up and eat. I know it is difficult because we have grown up in this world and that is how we have grown accustomed to using these platforms. Although this is true, for you to break the habit, you must set yourself up to get off these platforms quicker than you do right now. This could be true, or you could be getting more out of it by using it to truly network like how they were created to do. This will allow you to get the best of both worlds; you can spend your time on social media and get results from it at the same time.

The one true piss off is when people say they are busy all the time, but when a deadline comes for a project or an assignment or some sort of event, they aren't ready at all. What were they doing with the time they had? They were busy, were they not? How do they have to get all this work done in a short amount of time now if they were busy all the time before? That doesn't make sense at all. You can't be busy if you weren't doing anything, and the fact that you haven't been able to finish what you needed to get done clearly shows that. "But Taylor I'm busy all the time and I am still getting things done." Yes, that's true and I respect that, but is it meaningful things? Just because you're busy doesn't mean shit. Anyone can be busy. You could be busy all day buying groceries, shopping at the mall to get clothes you've needed for a while, dropping by your parents' house to say hi, or even cleaning your living room, kitchen, and bedroom. Those are all things that need to get done, but that doesn't mean you've done anything today. Those things haven't made your life move forward. If anything, you've brought yourself back by spending money on things you don't need (See chapter 5).

Now, if you can change this and do things that are meaningful to your life, you will feel much more accomplished no doubt. If you are currently working a job you love to do, then I would suggest going and getting more certified in it if that's possible. I would also search for people who are much better at your job or of a higher position and set up meeting with them to learn from them. This would only mean an enhancement in your performance, which is great for you and your employer. This is such a simple task, but not a lot of people are doing it. If you're in a job you hate, then you obviously do not want to be getting more certified in it. That's obvious. From listening to people like E.T. (featured in Chapter 5) and Gary, I've learned that making the most of your time after you're at that job is the best thing you can do. If you can make use of the 7pm-2am you're going to be spending more time doing what you love to do, rather than what you're not loving. This gives you the time to grow yourself in the sector that you want to be doing. If you can do this and use this time effectively, you're going to be at least starting to work towards a better situation for yourself.

I want you to be working towards what you want to be doing or becoming better in the job you're already at. This comes down to how you use your time. IF you're looking at the people who make upwards of $200,000+, they equal about 1% of people on the planet. It takes work. They don't get to come home and watch YouTube or TV for 4 hours and then take a nap. They must work 10-12 hours a day, minimum. Look at it like this. If you take the normal employee who works eight hours a day for 310 days a year (going with that number considering holidays, but that is still being generous), that means that they are working for about 2,400 hours a year. If you look at the person who is working 12 hours a day and loving the job they are at and is excelling, they are working for about 4,200 hours a year (Averaged at about 350 days of the year since they probably can work every day at what they love). That is the bare minimum. That doesn't take working weekends and extra hours into consideration. Now, that person working only eight hours isn't filling the same amount of time as the other are they.

I can honestly say that if you spend less time watching YouTube and sitting on the couch watching a TV show or playing games on your phone WHILE watching the TV, you will find yourself in some sort of better position than you were in before. Whether that be that you find yourself more productive in your job or life. You find yourself being better with time management, or even just find yourself spending more time doing what you love, even if you aren't making any money out of it. I know this chapter has sounded like a rant, but I want you to know that if you spend more of your time being productive and getting meaningful things that improve your life done, the happier you'll be.

Questions:

Are you currently busy all the time?

Is what you are doing productive towards your goals?

How can you change them if they aren't?

15

Go Work for Free

Why the hell would I work for free…?

Well, let me try and explain that in this chapter. I have met some great entrepreneurs so far in my life. Russ Rossi, the owner of On-Track, which is an online learning platform for employees who don't want to admit to their boss they don't know something. He has offices in Vancouver, Las Vegas, London, and New York. This man obviously knows what he is doing.

When I met with him at his office in Vancouver this past March, we talked about many things. He gave me insight into just what being an entrepreneur means and what it takes to be one. He talked to me about his life and how he grew up. Also, about what setting goals means to him and why he thinks it's very important to do. Although all this is true, he made a point that reassured what I was doing already myself. This was that the quickest way to get into doing what you want to be doing; working for free. What this means is that you go to a business or whoever you would work with for your business and tell them you will do everything for free. This allows you to work your way in because most likely they will be open to someone doing them a service for free. If you, for example, are someone who wants to start helping another business with their website. Do it for free. After you have helped them with it, you can ask them to be a reference for you in the future when you go and show other businesses what you have done for them. Now these businesses will most likely be able to pay you money for your efforts. This is because you were able to go to a business that is needing a new upgraded website and you're there to help for free.

Obviously doing a service for free doesn't make much logical sense. You should be getting paid for your time. If you look at the ROI of this, it's a better way of looking at it. From this one time of doing a service for free (or multiple times depending on what you need to do), it can allow you to go to a larger, more profitable business. Although you could do that, you can even go to the current businesses you are helping and ask for some sort of compensation going forward. This may take a couple months of work and letting them know that your services have been contributing a lot to the current state they are in.

Whichever route you take, it is always good to start off by creating value for the customer first, and then going with some sort of compensation later. This shows them that you are dedicated to what you are doing and have trust in yourself to get the job done. If you're doing something for free, you obviously want to be doing it. No one just does something for free because they hate it.

If you look at how hard sales people who work on commission work, you can get the picture. They are basically working for free until they get a sale. No money is in their hands until they create value for the people they are selling to (that's how you make a sale). They then create value for the company they work for (who pays them). That's why when you see a sales person work, they are attempting to talk to everyone they can making calls on calls. It takes a lot of work and they hopefully love what they are doing (if you want to make a lot of money doing that it should be based around what you love). Thinking about the money less when going to help someone with the service you are trying to sell to people will help a lot. If you take it to the point of this chapter and do it for free for someone first and possibly even more people, you will attract other customers and have reference for the ones you helped for free.

Working for free will be hard at first, and not an easy concept to understand – hence the first sentence of this chapter – but if you want to get your name out quickly and learn more about your sector, this can help a lot. Not many businesses are going to say no to something like this. Once again, if you can help someone for free and learn from what you are doing, the only long run effects of this are positive.

Questions:

Who could you help right now with what you love doing already?

What time of the day are you currently not making effective use of?

How long would you be able to work for free for?

How would you create value for someone with these free services?

16

Shed Your Insecurities

Everyone on this planet is insecure about something or gets anxious. I want to help you with this. Since everyone has them, it becomes a lot easier to think that it's just a normal habit to have these. You will think that it is perfectly fine and that you should never attempt to get rid of them. Your parents and friends won't push you to change them because they want to respect your thoughts on it.

That is where the problem begins. Fortunately for you, it isn't where it must end. We all can get wrapped into this, as I have as well. I struggled with this my whole life. I wasn't the most fit kid growing up and was a little bit overweight. This came with the normal problems of being bullied in school. I never felt that I could fit in with people being myself, so I went through stages of pretending to be someone who I wasn't. I found myself in situations that I never would have thought to be in. I always thought that I had to go to parties to be with the popular kids, but I quickly found out that it wasn't my thing. This was a big problem for me. I was a bit overweight until the age of 16, and then looked in the mirror one day and knew that I wasn't happy. I then started to go to the gym more often and cut out the food that wasn't good for me (this was quite a lot of food... I was eating four waffles every morning with each square filled with syrup). I felt very insecure about myself. Being able to put this into my book and put it on notice really shows just how much things change over time.

Many insecurities aren't just about weight. They're about facial features, school, being a "nerd", not hitting puberty like everyone else, not being a "nerd", not fitting in, and many more. These are okay. You're not defined by these and shouldn't let people make it seem like you are. In fact, these make you who you are, and you are amazing.

With the new movements being done by the younger generation, it is becoming easier to be open about yourself. Despite this, we still aren't open about ourselves and are able to be as transparent with others as we should be. I want you to know that you should talk about these things. The harder the conversation, the better you will feel after it is over, and the weight is lifted off your chest.

Sometimes this isn't just about having the conversation. It can be about getting over your fears as well. You may just need to go jump out of a plane. Yes, that's totally weird, but very true. Will Smith has a very popular interview where he goes on about a story about a time that he went skydiving. You can catch this on YouTube if you just look up "Will Smith Skydiving". I have listened to this video a ton of times. I sometimes listen to it if I start to feel nervous about something or get into a state of fear when I shouldn't be. What he talks about in the interview (a very funny one as usually, but still very serious), was how he was with his friends one night in Dubai and they made up the idea to go skydiving. Will trying not to kill the mood of course said yes to it. He then spent the rest of the night and the morning getting very anxious about it, and it was ruining his day, yet he hadn't done anything yet or even stepped onto the plane yet. They then went to the plane and he realized that it was really about to happen. He obviously was still very anxious since he had never done such a thing before. They started climbing in the air and he knew that it was soon coming; that he was going to have to jump out. When the door opened on the plane, he realized he had never been in a plane with the door open before. When he was the one up to go, he was pushed out on the count of two instead of three because people tend to grab on three. As soon as he was out of the plane and into the air, he felt complete bliss. Everything he felt before was completely gone and he felt no anxiety at all. So, what was the reason for this?

You get anxious about something you think about because you're thinking about all the negatives about it. Fear is just something we imagine it is, not what it's really going to be. In this case, Will Smith had thought about the worst parts of it, obviously the big one which is jumping out of a plane and dying. That wasn't rational thinking. He realized as soon as he jumped out that it was the complete opposite. It was the best experience of his life, and he would soon go even more times after. On the other side of fear, is everything we ever wanted. You fear getting that new job because it may be hard for you to handle, yet you're not even in the position yet, nor do you know what it feels to be in it yet. That is something I like to call False Fear. It is basically false thinking, but my own spin on it. The more you think you can't and put that thought of fear into your head, the more it manifests and takes over you. Like Will says in the interview, fear is just a thought we put into our head. It isn't naturally there since we put it into our own heads. I want you to go do one thing you're afraid of doing; it can be anything. It doesn't have to be a huge thing like jumping out of a plane. You can go to the gym for the first time in a while; you can tell someone how you feel about something because you feared how they would take it. You can do anything you feared doing before and see how you feel after. Remember, the best things in life are on the other side of fear. So, shed those insecurities and don't fear anything.

I also want to put here that I understand people do have a hard time with a lot of these things and it can escalate. So, if you do have any problems that you do struggle with, don't be afraid to message me on social media or email me. I would be happy to talk with you. Also talk to your doctor or a counselor and any other professionals that can help. You can also call 1-800-273-8255 if you're needing immediate help.

Questions:

What are you afraid of?

What is making your life not what you want it to be, and how are you going to change that?

17

Start to Hustle

Now that you're this far into the book, you're more than likely to listen to what I have to say in this chapter. You've been exposed to great tips like EQ, creating goals, and being yourself. With that, we move into hustling. Hustling isn't easy. It's going to be hard at first since you won't be as used to it. Hustling doesn't mean you work for all the hours of the day. To start you can take it small and do some extra work you don't usually do each day. Hustling and the word "working" go hand in hand. Putting in the work is going to help you. I can't stress that enough. Me being 20 years old, I know that even though I am in school right now, it doesn't mean I just turn off trying to start my own business, going to networking events, spending time learning and reading, and most of all hustling every damn day.

For People Not in A Job They Love (Read)

What are you doing with the time you aren't at this job? Are you spending it on the couch? Or better yet are you a student at school and not currently even working yet? What you are being taught isn't even something you want to do with your life. This goes for both the job and student. What are you doing with the time you have not doing these things. Can you spend it doing what you love? Can you grind that shit out at work and turn it into a career path and something you can live off? (You need shelter and it doesn't have to be all paid by you, live in a basement suite with some friends if you must).

Some of the greatest things have come from people who had a business on the side. Some people had to work two jobs and then work on what they loved. Logic is a perfect example of this. If you don't know who that is, it takes a simple google search. He spent his time rapping and making songs after he came home from working two jobs. This man worked two jobs and then would come home and go work on his actual craft.

He now is one of the most well-known music artists on the planet and was nominated for a Grammy for best song of the year. That's an incredible journey. For those of you who don't feel that you are in a job that you love, I hope that this helps you take on something new that you do love you start creating something with it.

For People in A Job They Love (Read)

Why aren't you going after it 100%? Have you ever heard of the phrase "Work in your job, not on your job?" That should resonate with you. If you are just spending your time going to work and not actually being a part of the company, just doing whatever they need of you and not taking it to some sort of other level, you're not being your best self. Even if you are not an entrepreneur and instead you're just working for a business and helping it out, that doesn't mean you don't become a part of it if you love what you're doing. Throw yourself at it and let it become a bigger part of your life. Who knows, maybe something amazing will come of it. I would hope that the business you work at would recognize this and know that you are doing more than the average worker.

I don't understand someone that loves what they are doing, but don't want to work on it longer than the 40-hour work week. How do you claim that you love it, yet you're not spending extra time that you could on it and instead are doing dumb shit that is a waste of time (I would hope you're not)? You love your spouse that you will end up living your whole life with and would spend time with even when you know you've spent a ton of time with them. So why not do this with your job as well? Why are you holding yourself back from getting a raise, or taking your career to the next level? That's all your own doing. I have touched on this before, so I won't keep hounding you with that fact.

Okay I lied, I totally am.

You are the person who shapes yourself. So, spend that extra hour a day working on a project at your work. Make that extra effort that no one else is making because you love what you're doing. This hopefully only is making more sense as to why you should do this. If you aren't willing to hustle, or to get to work (exact same thing, I know), then what are you doing? Why are you letting your days pass by without making sure something is being done, or you're progressing your life to where you see yourself to be. Make use of this time you have and keep the hustle alive. This can be started as easily as right now. If you think you know how you can start right now and want to make that effort, put this god damn book down and get out there. I want you to fucking do it. Get up and go. If you still are unsure and want to learn more, then continue reading this, and if you need to read again, do it. You just need to know that once you have that itch to go and hustle, go out and get after it.

Questions:

What does hustling mean to you?

How can you make sure you are not just sitting around?

Will you make incremental changes each day to your life?

18

Have a Sense of Urgency

Don't you just hate it when you ask someone to help you do something, and then they take their sweet ass time. Well that's what this chapter is, but it's about the fact that you say you're going to do something, and then take your sweet ass time.

So, you want to change up your life? Do you want to start setting goals? When is it going to happen? Are you going to remember tomorrow when you wake up to set some goals for the day? Are you going to go buy a blackboard, so you can write all of them down? These are questions you need to answer, just like how you need to be able to answer, "In the next 24 hours I am going to…." because if you wait any more than that to do this, you have already lost. Most people will forget that feeling they had when you decide to start bettering your life when a day or so passes by. This comes from the fact that you think that it is impossible now for you to achieve what you wanted to do. I hate that.

Having a sense of urgency makes that feeling of not being able to do something, or the second guessing of yourself, go away for the time being (I say this because you will encounter that feeling, but you're going to learn to brush it off). When it comes to me, I am always in attack mode. If I think of an idea, I write it down right away. If I need to get a hold of someone about something, I call them right away and don't wait. I also make sure that if I have important work to be done, that I get it done right in the morning because that way it is done and now the rest of the day is devoted to the other things that help with what I am doing. As soon as I had an idea for this book, I wrote down every chapter idea I had and then started writing it. I didn't say to myself that I could wait until tomorrow or the next day. I stopped what I was doing and started writing it. It's that sense of urgency that is going to make or break you.

I have met a lot of people without this. They tend to tick me off a bit. You will find that when you develop this, you will be able to tell when people simply don't practice the same thing. You will find others to be late when you're early and you will find people you're close to never getting what you need done right away done. You won't be receiving the same sense of urgency you give out because people simply don't see it that way. We take for granted when someone does this for us. Think about it, when you last had something done for you at a restaurant or another establishment. When the food came out quick for you, did you thank the chef and let them know you were happy to get it so quick? Or did you just shrug it off and think to yourself that it is how it should be? If it is the latter you're being truthful.

As for the people I do know that do practice this, I love it. I have a friend who I was helping work on his goal setting and we worked on it from midnight until 230am. This was a very in-depth conversation and I was really hoping he would spend the next day continuing to do the things that were talked about. This held true and I could tell that he was making sure he was using a sense of urgency and wanted to get going on what he was doing. That would not have been able to happen if he didn't find that urgency that we both knew was in him. If he had left that out and not really cared about making sure he set his goals, he would have just reverted to exactly how he was the day before, no problem. The fact that I can say "no problem" is horrible.

Obviously, it may be hard to just do everything like this. You shouldn't be trying to go to the washroom with a sense of urgency, that's for sure. You can start small. This would involve just getting your daily tasks done, but quicker. If you empty your dishwasher in 10 minutes, make it 5. If you have certain tasks at your job that you normally do, try and get them done a bit quicker than usual. This will help create that idea in your mind that you need to get things done. This will help you grow into the person who acts with urgency. Look at someone like Gary Vee or Grant Cardone. They are highly successful because they act with urgency. They know that they need to get things done and that involves making sure it's done right away instead of pushing it off. When Grant Cardone first started selling, he could have left trying to 10X everything until he was truly into the car selling market, which really made a name for himself. When I say 10X, that's his rule. What it means is, is that if you make 10 phone calls one day for your sales job, then make 100 the next. Even if you're not in sales, just try to do a ton more than what you would usually do to see some success from it. Instead, he decided that he was going to do it to make a name for himself. See what happened there? His sense of urgency to start doing what he said he should be doing right away lead him to start doing better at his job.

There are not many other better ways to see results quicker in your life than practicing this. Making your thoughts into reality is always a great thing. From my own personal experience with this, it is always better to have a sense of urgency. I am what I am because I never pushed things to the side, and instead went directly at them. You probably hear from people that doing that is bad for you, so I hope this chapter has changed your mind. I hope you can write down some goals and go out and achieve them tomorrow. You deserve the very best and this is a part of your journey to get there. So next time you have something you should be getting done, get it the fuck done.

Questions:

What can you do a bit quicker starting tomorrow?

What does 10X mean?

What part of your life should you have more urgency about? Do you have any ideas you have put off?

Why can having a sense of urgency help your life?

19

Create Your Blueprint

This is the lovely old saying of getting rid of your shitty habits that you don't want anymore. Those habits that you would love to have gone, but still always end up doing because you feel more comfortable doing them. That's exactly it; you're being comfortable. Stop being so comfortable. Get it through your head that you are supposed to be comfortable with being uncomfortable. This is probably the most used word ever when it comes to motivation. In this case, to really get your habits into how you want them to be, you need to create a blueprint that fits into a positive lifestyle.

This is a term used and taught by Tony Robbins. He talks about it in a way that really changes how people perceive themselves and ends up finding joy out of every day. Now, if you don't currently have a life blueprint, that is totally fine. It would make sense. At the end of this chapter, there will be a page dedicated for you to start writing out what you want your life to be like. This should include the following:

- Your end goal of where you want to be (i.e. Financial Freedom, Known person, etc.)
- What you want your life right now to be
- What your passions are
- What would make you the happiest that isn't related to money

Having these written down helps you feel more successful when you reach them. If you have achievements and life goals set out and you feel as though you are at them, then when you look at these you're going to feel quite fulfilled. Now, that's a lot better than thinking your life isn't what you thought it would be, that's for sure. Meeting your own expectations is a great achievement because those are set out by you and not someone else. This blueprint can help you do that. Tony also talks about the opposite of this, and that is the people who don't typically do this and don't see a reason to. They usually aren't too happy with their lives because they aren't sitting where they want to be. They have the ideas of what they want to be but aren't taking the steps to get to those ideas. You don't want to be unhappy, do you? If you currently are, hopefully you can realize that you just need to take some simple steps to start feeling better. Then lay out this sort of blueprint to help do that for you.

As you create a blueprint for yourself, you should be looking at the things you give the most time to. This shows you all the things you're most comfortable with. That makes sense. Why wouldn't you just do all the things that make you feel comfortable? This makes you put all the time that you should be spending learning new things and putting yourself into a position where you won't be able to get out of your bad habits. If you become too comfortable in an environment where your bad habits are a part of that, then you won't be able to get yourself out. That is until you change your mindset and create a blueprint that allows you to take yourself to a new level.

Part of the reason why this self-blueprint is so useful is that it gives you a direction. The saying goes, "The good life is a process, not a state of being. It is a direction not a destination." – Carl Rodgers. Having a direction and knowledge of who you are is what makes you different from Joe Bob. The more you know about yourself and where you want to go, means you have a better idea of how to take yourself to the next level. If you don't have a direction, how are you supposed to get to where you want to go? I have never met someone who has a direction of where they want their life to go, and are on that journey, who is unhappy or doesn't enjoy their life. They are ecstatic that every single day they are working towards what they want and are who they mapped themselves out to be. Don't you want that as well? Why do all the people that become successful preach that you can be happy do these things? Just find out who you are.

It is sad to say, but many of the people who aren't happy are usually the ones working jobs that aren't really a reflection of the self-blueprint they have created for themselves. They are going against who they want to be and struggle with that. That's why on the weekends they want nothing to do with the work they do, and it wouldn't be an option to talk about that with them. They will not usually converse about work and don't usually bring it up. Now ask yourself the question

Is that what you want to be?

Or would you rather be the one out of everyone that always brings out how your life is and what you're doing? Will you let people know where you are and that you are truly happy? Why can't you be that? What is holding you back? If you think it's anything but yourself, you're wrong. Go and create your self-blueprint and start taking your life into your own hands. Be the person people look at for help or knowledge. Nothing is stopping you from doing that, but the idea you have in your head says you can't. I could have given up everything when I was at SFU with a .4 GPA. I could have blamed anyone but myself. Instead I looked at what I was doing wrong and searched for who I wanted to be and created an idea of where I wanted to go. This has led me to writing this book right now for you to do the same and take your own life to the next level.

Questions:

What is your end goal in life?

20

Go Have Experiences

Now, you've made it this far. You're on the final tip that I am going to give you before you head off and do what you feel needs to be done. Whatever that may be, do the best you possibly can.

Let's get down to business because I'm sure at this point, you're tired of reading this book and just want to finish it off (Rebecca I'm talking to you). So, what is an experience? Is it going for a trip to your dream destination? Doing everything you've always wanted to do before? Jumping out of a plane? Spending a year abroad to learn new cultures? Well, it's all these things. It's vital you don't drown yourself in work all the time because you're going to get to the point where you're sick of it. Especially if you spend every single day from your 20's until your 30's always grinding. This wouldn't be good if you spent that time working for someone else who will never give you the recognition for it either.

Go and have some life experiences first. When you're young, it is easier for you to just get up and go somewhere. You're not tied down by anything, and even if you are, figure it out. Nothing should hold you back from living the life you want to live. If you have always dreamed of going to Australia for five months, go fucking do it. Why not? Who's holding you back? Your girlfriend or boyfriend? Parents? Boss? Why do they have so much control over you? Isn't it your life? Since when did it become theirs to say what you can and can't do. Even if you need to get a job there making under the table cash, go for it.

Would you be happy when you're 40 years old and knowing that even if you went and did that one thing you have always wanted to do, you would still be in the same place you are now. You could also be happier knowing you did it. I know for a fact that as a 40-year-old, you wouldn't be happy about that. I get having a family and getting that house is what everyone wants, and you should be happy you even have that, but why not go and do what you want to do? Why do you have to think of yourself when you're 40 and not having been able to go for a 5-month long trip?

So many people who grind and want to be someone forget that those people are super happy doing what they are doing. Jeff Bezos is probably the cheeriest guy around. The question is would you be happy doing what you're doing even though you'll never get the chance to go and do something you can do right now? If you're afraid of losing your minimum wage job that you work three times a week at while in school, then get outside yourself. There are a million minimum wage jobs around and you can always get another one.

You might think it costs a lot of money to go for what you want to do. Think about it like this. When you're working your job, and you're not as happy as you could be, how much is that costing you? Well it's costing you the extra hours you would have stayed because you love life, it's costing you those extra fights you have with your spouse because you're blaming her/him for something that was in your own control, it's costing you the other self that you could have been.

Please stop letting others hold you back. No matter what your position in life is. If you don't have a car, money, or even that great of a family. Why don't you just go out and have the experience that will resonate throughout your whole life? I plan on going skydiving and going to Italy as soon as I can. I have also already gone through a ton of experiences and am happier because of it. I have been to the Big Apple and to California. I have spent time enjoying the fact that I am alive, and that you to should do as well. The more you realize that the more time you spend pushing that trip, or experience off, the less happy you are going to be. Does it feel good having to leave it until the next year because you couldn't find time last year to do it? I hope not.

All I am trying to say is that you're alive. And some of you may be 24, or 27. Maybe you're even 30 and reading this. You could be 15 and come across this book (that would be so awesome). It doesn't matter how old you are. What matters is that you take your life in your own hands.

Like I have said before, the chances of you being alive is 400 Trillion to 1. That's some shitty odds. Except you won it. You did it. You're alive. So, stop making excuses for dumb shit and be you. Have experiences, get work done, and live the amazing life that you deserve. Every day is a blessing and a half. Everyone can wake up and live the life they want to. It isn't on your mother or your father to make sure of that. It's on you. So, start living life on your terms and make sure that every second you're alive contains these tips I have given you. They might not be the most in-depth, this book may not be 500 pages long, but trust in me that if you think about these tips daily, you can live a better life than you are right now. I thank you so much for reading my book. This means so much to me and I hope you can be the person you want to be. I leave you with a quote by Ralph Emerson that speaks so much wisdom.

"Go where no one has gone before and leave a trail."

—Ralph Emerson

Questions:

What do you want to do in the next 3 months that you have never done before? (i.e. Skydiving for example)

What experiences have you had in your life that you had an amazing time doing that you have forgotten about?

How did that experience make you feel?

Final Tip

Always Reflect

I want you to reflect about what you've learnt in this book. If it has changed how you thought about your actions daily or has inspired any general thoughts you have about what you want to do starting tomorrow.

DO NOT FLIP PAGE UNTIL AFTER

Here are some of the things I reflect on after writing this book. This book changed how I see my daily life. Even with me already knowing all the topics covered, I still learned a lot after going through each one and making sure that each one is vital in my life. I would catch myself during the day doing something I shouldn't because the book was keeping me accountable for my actions. I can't write this book for all of you and then simply not do what I said you should. Also stick to the fact that you can't go and rewrite what you just wrote. What I have written here is totally raw and hasn't been revised or edited at all. This is 100% written at my desk without having a second look.

After going through the past 7 months of getting this book out for everyone to read, I realized that my life has changed even since then. I decided to start my own agency and took on a summer job that I had no idea if it would work but tried it anyway instead of getting a sure thing. When I first started writing this book, it didn't feel the same as when I did the last 75% of the book. I found this drive to make sure I got it out to anyone that took the time to read it. I would find myself getting so into writing that I wasn't even aware of the music I was listening to.

I find myself in a different place. I think that's the best thing I could say. What I mean by that is that even though you find yourself in a better place right now, you're going to find yourself in an even better place in the next month, or six months, or even a year. Does that make sense to you? As you keep applying these things across your life, you're always going to be making incremental improvements and finding new ways to better yourself. That's what's really cool about all this, that even when you do find a great spot and you could totally stop right there, you will still be able make even more improvements on top of that.

I hope this book has helped you as much as it has helped me. Now, it's your time to go and kill it. Remember to be yourself and not care when people put you down. Get at these tips each day and do what you need to do.

This is a list of books that I think would be great for you to read. They all talk about how you can become a better persona and understanding yourself.

Reading List:

Gary Vaynerchuk

- Crush It
- Thank You Economy
- Jab, Jab, Jab, Right Hook
- #AskGaryVee
- Crushing It

Tony Robbins

- Awaken The Giant Within
- Unshakeable: Your Financial Freedom Playbook

Dale Carnegie

- How to Win Friends and Influence People
- How to Stop Worrying and Start Living

Paulo Coelho

- The Alchemist

Ray Dalio

- Principles

Travis Bradberry and Jean Greaves

- Emotional Intelligence 2.0

Stephen R. Covey

- The 7 Habits of Highly Effective People

Thank You for Reading

Made in the USA
San Bernardino, CA
27 July 2018